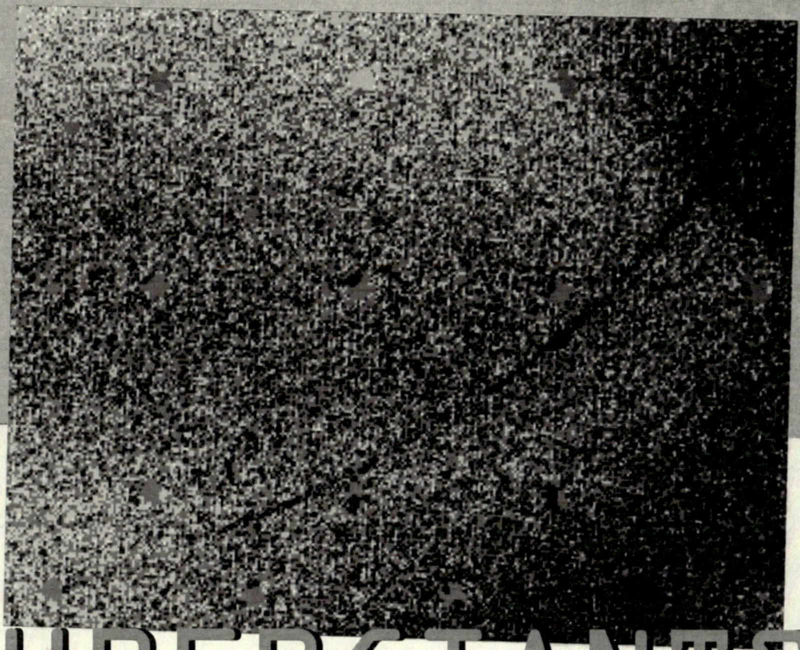

SUPERGIANTS

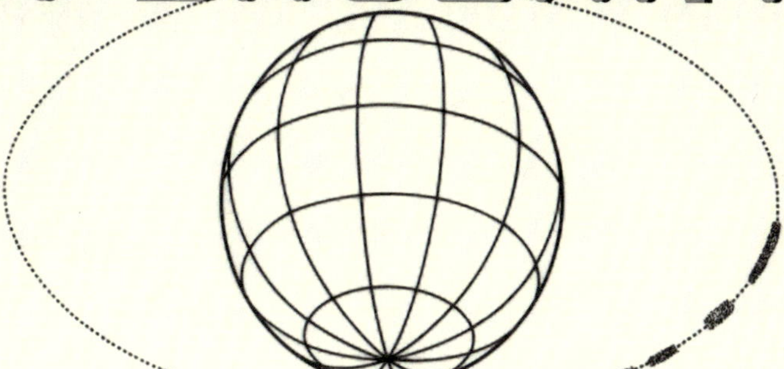

POEMS

KYLE FLEMMER

Also by Kyle Flemmer

Barcode Poems

KYLE FLEMMER

SUPERGIANTS

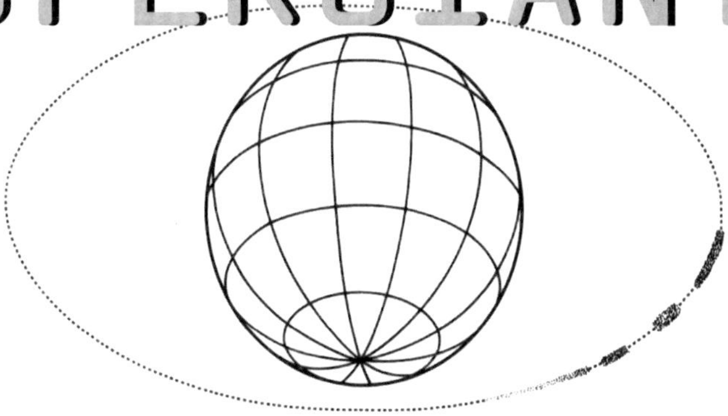

A Buckrider Book

Published by Buckrider Books
an imprint of Wolsak and Wynn Publishers
280 James Street North
Hamilton, ON L8R2L3
www.wolsakandwynn.ca

Editor: Paul Vermeersch | Copy editor: Ashley Hisson
Cover and interior design: Kilby Smith-McGregor
Author photograph: Sarah Thomas
Typeset in Courier Prime, Courier New, and OCR A Std
Printed by Coach House Printing Company, Toronto, Canada

The publisher gratefully acknowledges the support of the Canada Council for the Arts and the Ontario Arts Council. We also acknowledge the financial support of the Government of Canada through the Canada Book Fund and the Government of Ontario through the Ontario Book Publishing Tax Credit and Ontario Creates.

Library and Archives Canada Cataloguing in Publication

Title: Supergiants / Kyle Flemmer.
Names: Flemmer, Kyle, author.
Identifiers: Canadiana 20250154137 | ISBN 9781998408146 (softcover)
Subjects: LCGFT: Poetry.
Classification: LCC PS8611.L436 S87 2025 | DDC C811/.6—dc23

Knee-deep in the cosmic overwhelm ...

Diane Ackerman
"Diffraction"

There is imperative –
a cause, a god. Or not.

Alice Major
"Let us compare cosmologies"

FOR C.V.

*

CONTENTS_

When I first looked up
at the midnight sky I saw
points not constellations

* * * * * * *

When I was a child
the stars rained down
on my imagination

* * * * *

When I looked as man
I saw the patterns
others wanted me to see

* * *

When I grew old
my milky eyes
beheld no galaxies

*

And as I die
the stars go out

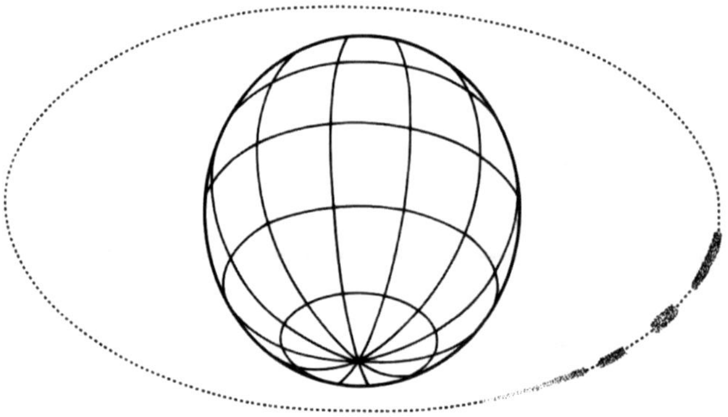

MODULAR SYSTEMS_

PHOTOGRAPHIC MODULE
COMMAND TASKS

Observation during
zodiacal libration

Lunar command
of Earth

Starlight through sextant:
in through the

Near side lunar module
Moon the L4 sextant module

Specific solar corona segments
Earthshine by region

Dark surface fields
eclipse the light

Galactic command
Earth terminator

MODULAR SYSTEMS

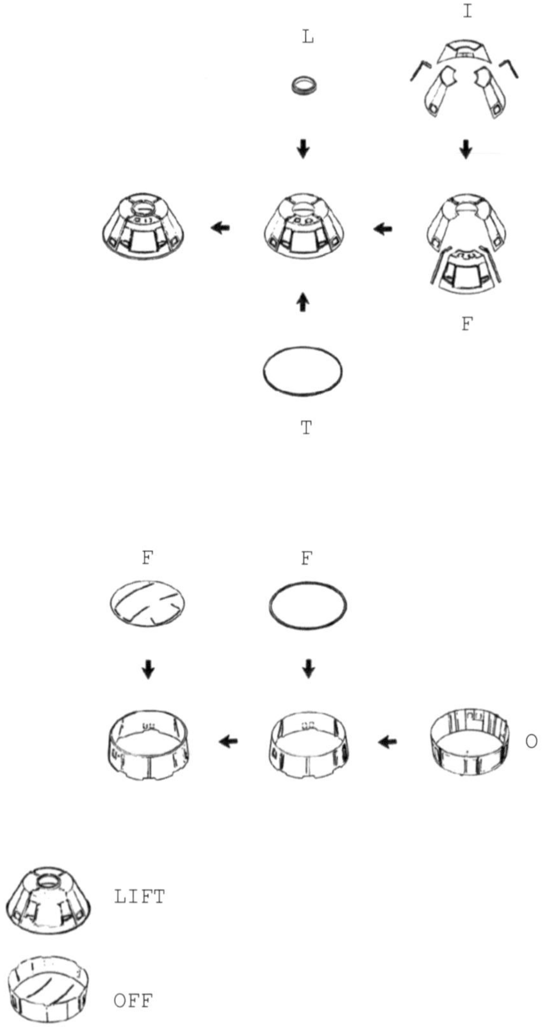

fig. 1

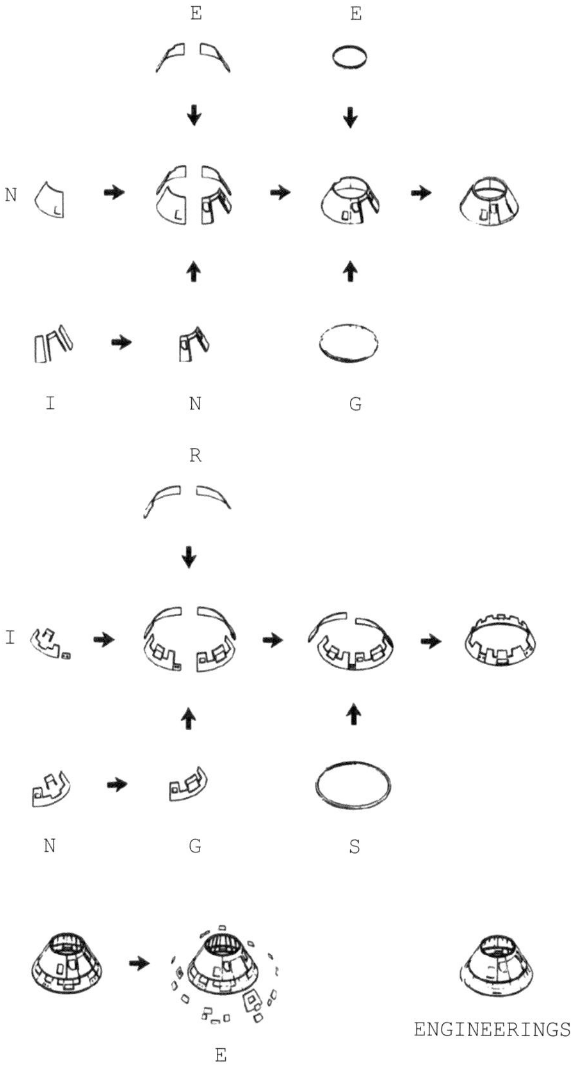

fig. 2

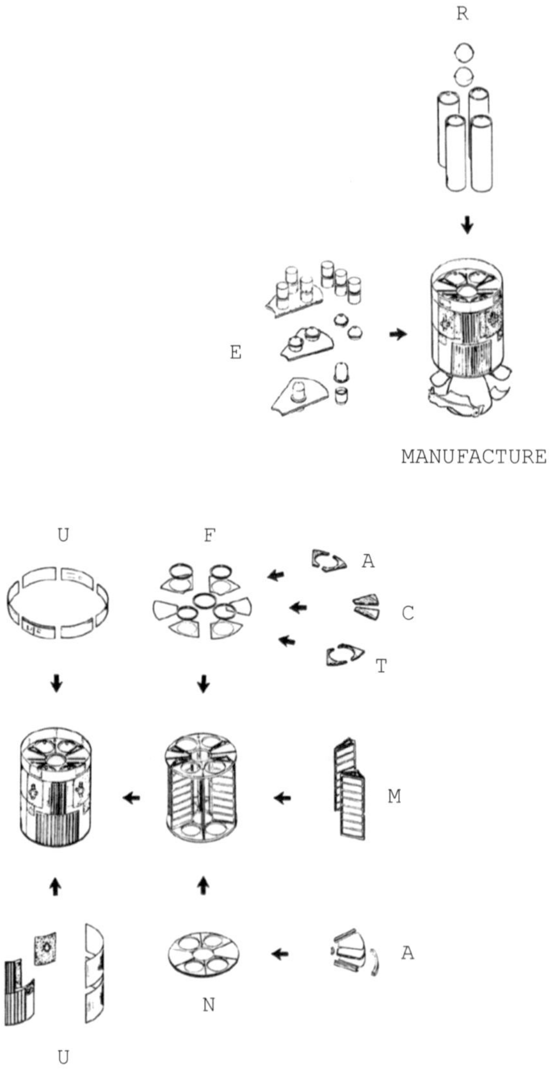

fig. 3

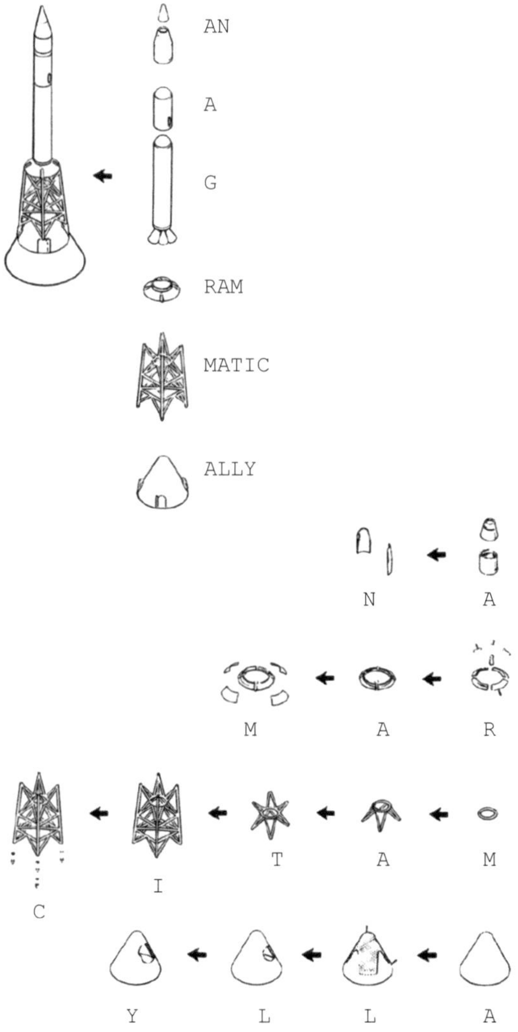

fig. 4

BLUE DOT PALE

one ship scaling an open sky
remaking other solar frontiers

wanderers among great darkness
protecting sacred life on moons

Apollo tiptoeing through heaven
Voyager exploring new planets

interplanetary acknowledgements
black Earth a Milky Way demotion

Camarina is light made triumph
universe of routine violence!

this marsh melts world ground
you index planet aberrations

morning at first introduction
evening to Saturn references

wonder not for star gates
gift us American contents

worlds here and there:
are the system intelligent?

BASIC VOCABULARY FOR SUBSEQUENT READING

readers should be familiar with the following terms:

curved connective space eclipse,
annular star latitude index,
object W elliptic motion system,
irregular galactic proton pressure,
astronomical albedo unit density,
minor spectroheliogram spicules,
right prime velocity precession,
normal stellar photon wavelengths,
chromatic neutron equator pole,
photographic Tauri orbit curve,
Canis Majoris fireball star,
equator line eclipse aberration,
electron energy transition level,
heliocentric reference parallax,
Balmer spectrum supergiant star,
flare mass rotation scattering,
radioactive photosphere accretion,
metastable galactic latitude,
positively diffuse electron sphere,
spiral galaxy of peculiar light,
planetary half-life perihelion,
retrograde nucleus ionization,
Lyman series meteorite cluster,
galaxy limb escape velocity,
atomic matter zenith tides,
tangential coronae declination,
evolutionary Herbig-Haro galaxy,
autumnal comet light effect,
R dwarf zodiacal number,
continuous giant Doppler equinox,
absolute sunspot magnitude angle,
globular winter neap cluster,
aphelion meteor frame longitude,
T series Virginis nova star,
binary visual spectrograph granules,
summer gegenschein orbit velocity,
main parsec luminosity sequence,
Borealis RR Lyrae star shell,

emission spectrum fluorescence,
resolving star motion eclipse,
chromosphere beta prominence,
mare type electron spin velocity,
apparent angstrom color absorption,
parallax of degenerate magnitude,
red-shift zero curvature space,
population I continuum galaxy,
ecliptic diurnal mass types,
spectral limb power darkening,
true visual solstice revolution,
color eclipsing binary flare star,
total umbra envelope decay,
Balmer planet radiation pressure,
excess celestial star objects,
spectrum of apparent equinox,
vernal solstice line ascension,
solar plage reversing layer,
electromagnetic spectrum cosmology,
galactic lunar apogee association,
white light nebula track,
negatively curved geodesic emission,
synodic solar eclipse meridian,
focal spectrum objective length,
Cepheid magnitude celestial state,
apparent spectroscopic magnitude,
sidereal perigee solar period,
partial occultation eclipse penumbra,
barred spiral reflection nebula,
light magnitude protoplanet,
spectroscopic nebula parallax,
population II objects cosmogony,
the forbidden atomic longitude,
proper galactic velocity terminator,
ellipse broadening radial focus,
binary population curve space,
radioactive celestial star period,
and flash dark filament corona.

SPACE ACHIEVEMENTS

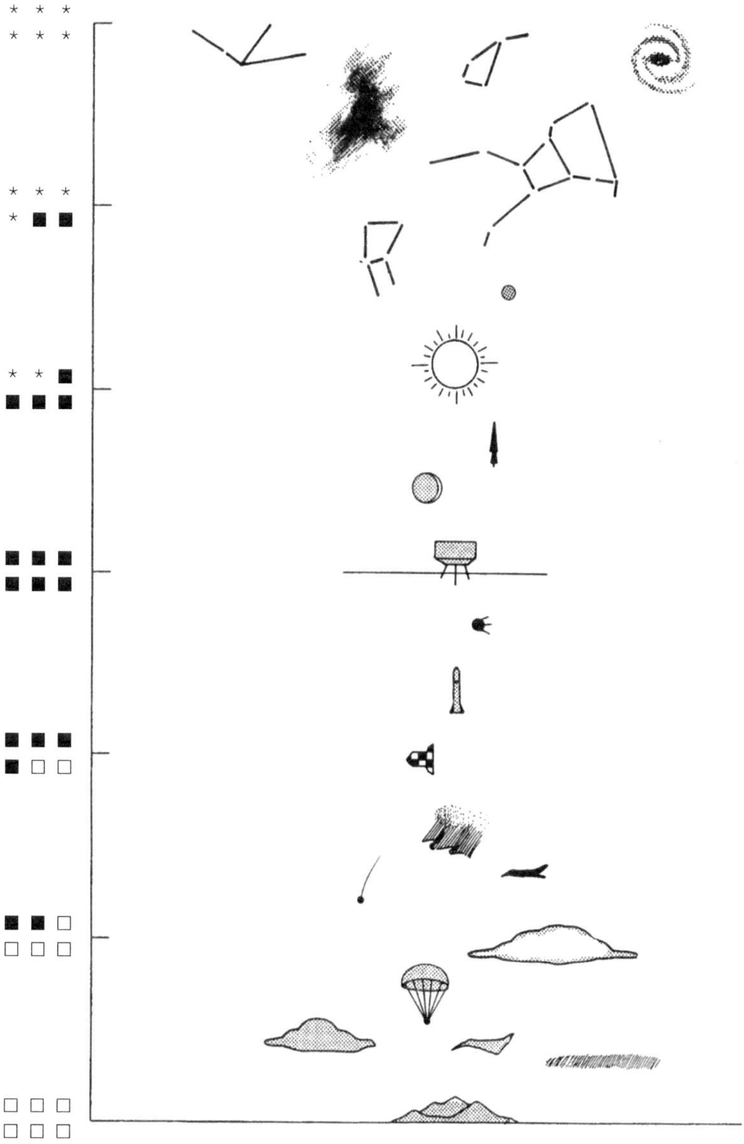

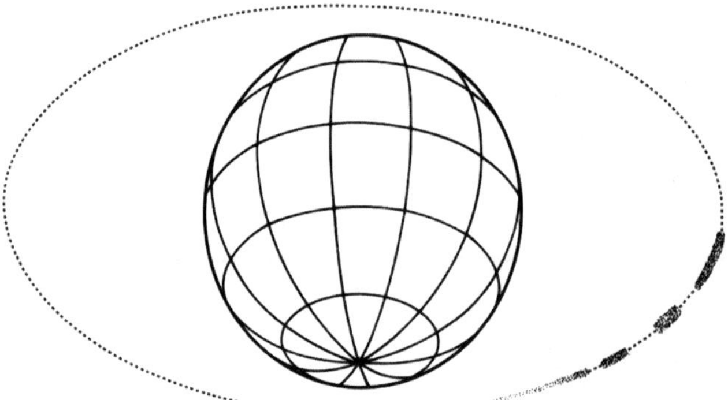

LUNAR FLAG ASSEMBLY KIT_

As we explore the reaches of space,
let us go to the new worlds together —
not as new worlds to be conquered,
but as a new adventure to be shared.

President Richard Nixon
Inaugural Address, 1969

XI.

July 20, 1969 Lunar Module (LM) *Eagle* performs the first crewed landing on the Moon their Lunar Flag Assembly (LFA) kit designed by NASA engineer Mr. Fix It contains telescoping tubes of anodized aluminum and a standard American flag even though the Outer Space Treaty forbid national claims over other worlds a flag planted in the Sea of Tranquility 8.2 m from the LM is blown over by exhaust from *Eagle*'s takeoff

□□□□□□□ □□□□□□□□□□□□□□□□□□□□□□
□□□□□□□□□□□□□□□□□□□□□□□□□□□□□□
□□□□□□□□□□□□□□□□□□□□□□□□□□□□□□
□□□□□□□□□□□□□□□□□□□□□□□□□□□□□□
□□ □□□□□□□□□□□□□□□□□□□□□ □□□□□
□□□□□□□□□□□□□□□□□□□□□□□□□□□□□□
□□□□□□□□□□□□□□□□□□□□□ □□□□□□□□
□□□□□□□□□□□□□□□□□□□□□□□□□□□□□□
□□□□□□□□ □□□□□□□ □□ □□□□□□□□□□
□□□□□□□□□□□□□□□□□□□□□□□□□□□□□□
□□□□□□□□□□ □□□□□□□□□□□□□ □□□□
□□□□□□□□□□□□□□□□□□□□□□□□□□□□□
□□□□□□□□□□□□□□□□□ □□□ □□□□□□□□
□□□□□□□□□□□□□□□□□□□□□□□□□□□□
□□□□□□□□□□□ □□□□ □□□□□ □□□
■
■
■
■
■
■
■
■
■
■
■
■
■
■
■
■
■
■
■
■
■
■
■
■
■
■
■

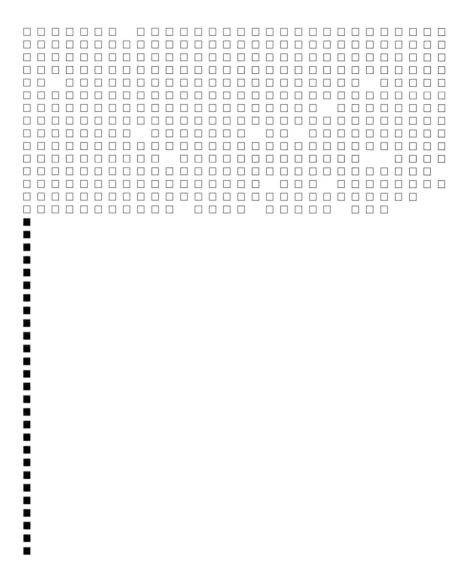

XII.

Congress declares lunar flags to be "symbolic gesture[s]
of national pride" in November 1969 as a lightning-
struck lander alights in the Ocean of Storms
their lunar television camera is damaged by the sun's
electromagnetic waves propagating at 300,000 km/s
regardless of wavelength or frequency the LFA kit is
deployed and though it weighs 6x less on the Moon
its horizontal latch pole fails to support the flag

□□□□□□□□□□□□□□□ □□□□□□□□□□□□□□
□□□□□□□□□□□□□□□□□□□□□□□□□□□□□
□□□□□□□□□   □□□□□□□□□□□   □□□□□□
□□□□□□□□□□□□□□□□□□□□□□□□□□□□□
□□□□□□□ □□□□□□   □□□□□□□□□□□
□□□□□□□□□□□□□□   □□□□□□□□□□□
□□□□□□□□□□□□□□□□   □□□□□□□□□□□□
□□□□□□□□□□□□□□□□□□ □□□□□□□
□□□□□□□□□□   □□□□□□□□□□□□□□□□□
□□□□□□□□□□□□□□□□□□□□□□□□□□□□□□
□□□□□□□□□□□□□ □□□□□□□□□□ □□□□□
□□□□   □□□□□□□□□□□□□□□□ □□□□
□□□□□ □□□□□□□□□□□□□□□□□□□□□□□
□□□□□□□□□□□□□□   □□□□□□□□□□□□
□□□□□□□□□□□□□   □□□□□□□□□□□□
■
■
■
■
■
■
■
■
■
■
■
■
■
■
■
■
■
■
■
■
■
■
■
■
■
■
■

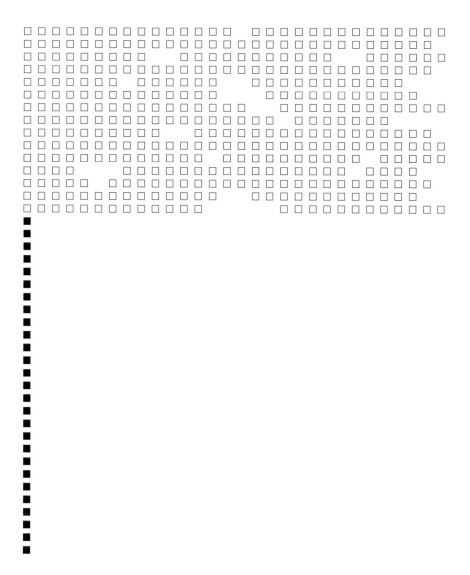

XIII.

an oxygen tank explodes on Apollo 13   crippling the
command and service module (CSM)   the LFA kit remains
strapped   to the external ladder of the LM   inside
an expensive thermal shield   ultraviolet radiation
breaks down   the chemical bonds   in dye molecules
landing is aborted   the mission takes a
circumlunar trajectory   400,000 km from Earth
and the farthest   anyone   has strayed   from home

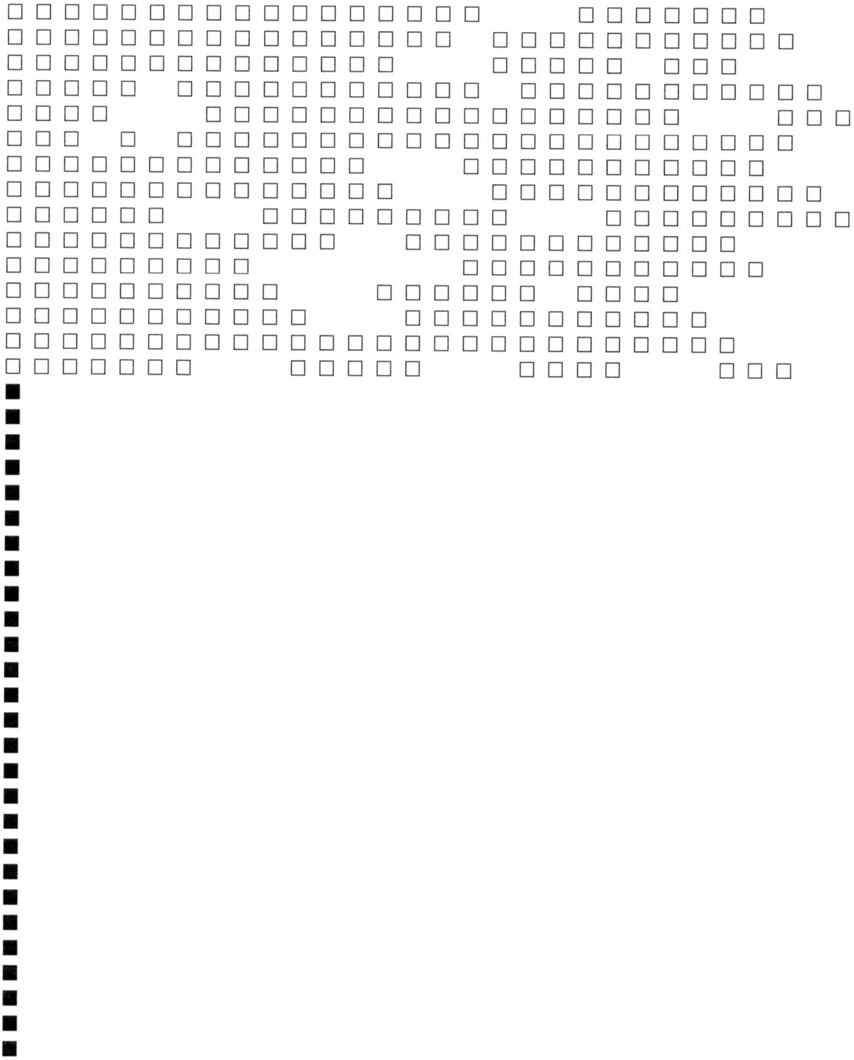

XIV.

despite docking problems   and a faulty abort switch
color footage   of the LFA kit   is returned
from   Fra Mauro   the flag cost $5.50   from a
government   supply catalog   unaltered
except   for a sleeve   sewn along   its top   hem
to accommodate   the horizontal   latch pole
once   unfurled   radiation   and   meteorites
gradually   degrade   the   flag

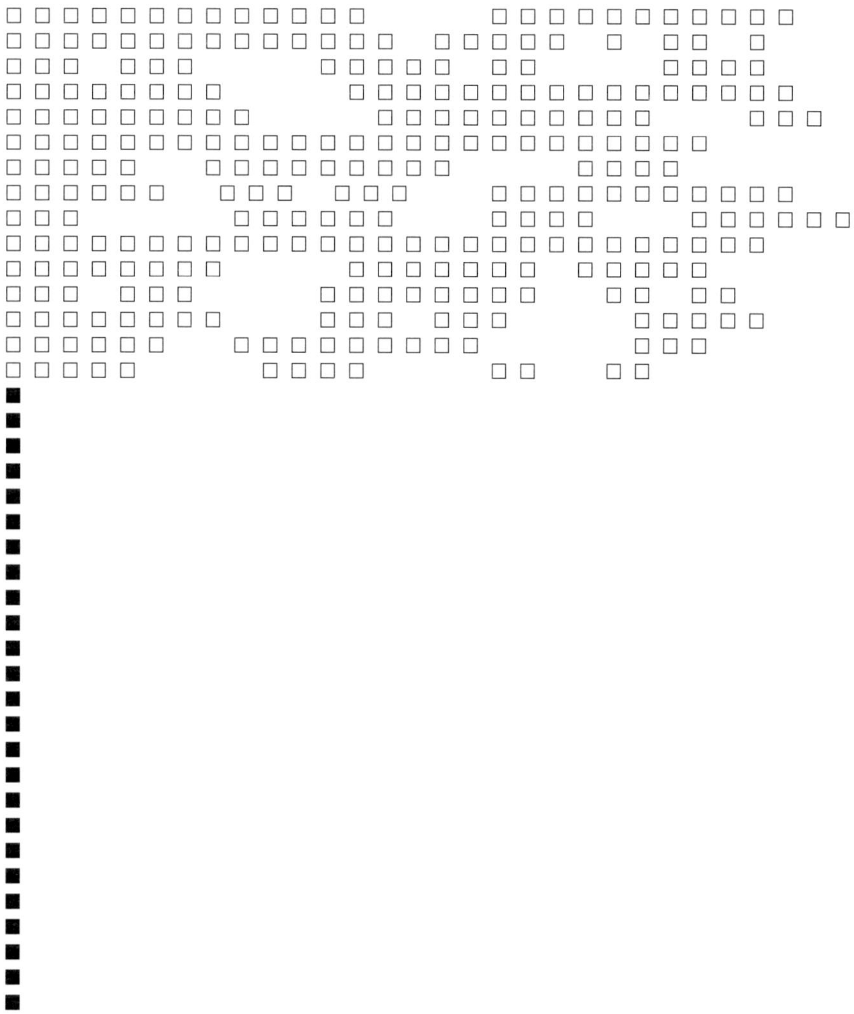

XV.

the first mission to emphasize
investigation and observation the J-Series
rocketeers put language to landscape
they make notes downlink their findings
by microwave and leave an aluminum statuette
to honor their dead the *Fallen Astronaut*
it drops 250°C in passing
from sunlight into shade

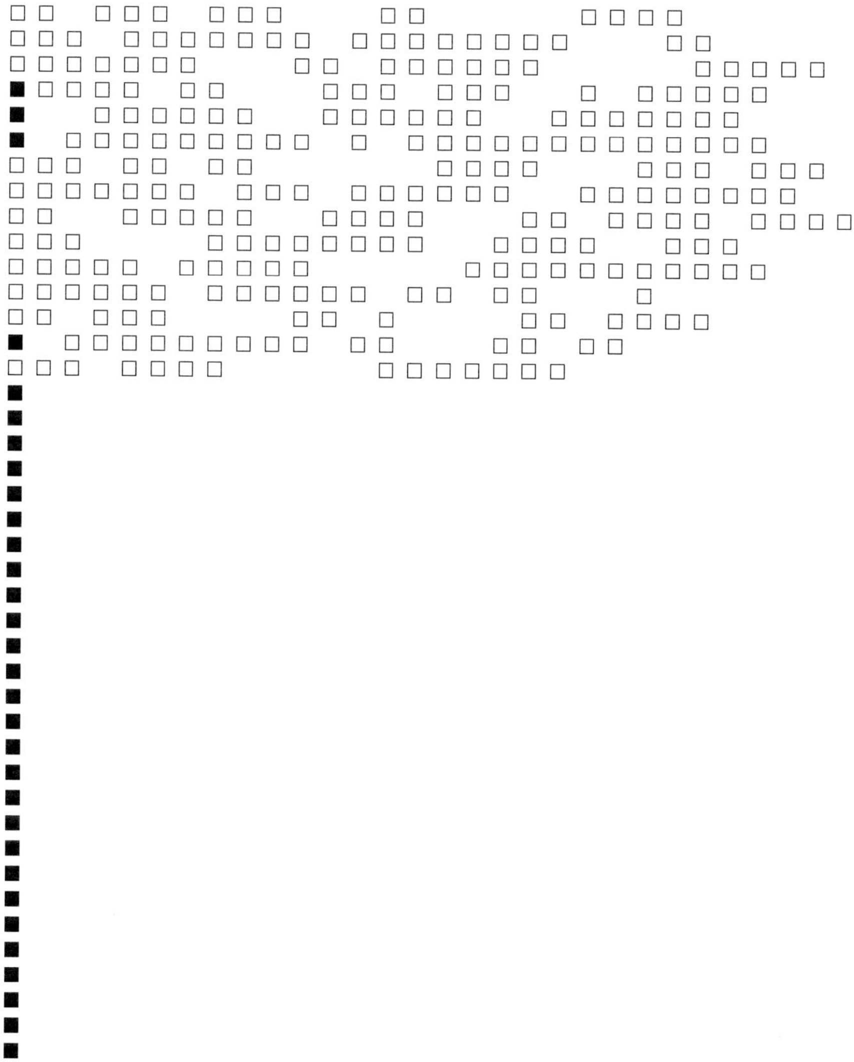

XVI.

a backup CSM yaw gimbal servo loop
malfunctions en route the LM's
steerable antenna is broken
white fabric reflects most light
in the visible spectrum
the lunar flags are bleached
one star frees fifty from each
raised stateless in abandon

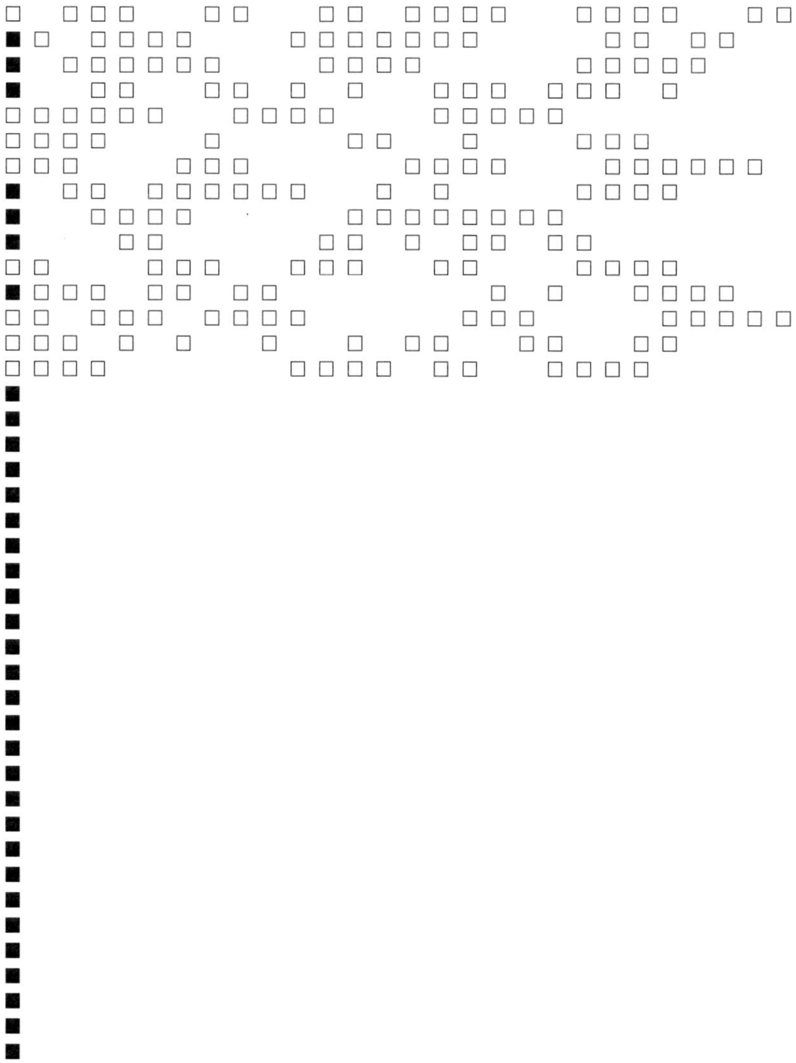

XVII.

the last moon flag
flew in Mission Control through
all prior missions photos
of the landing sites confirm
five of six flags still
fly their shadows
black against moondust
in white starlight

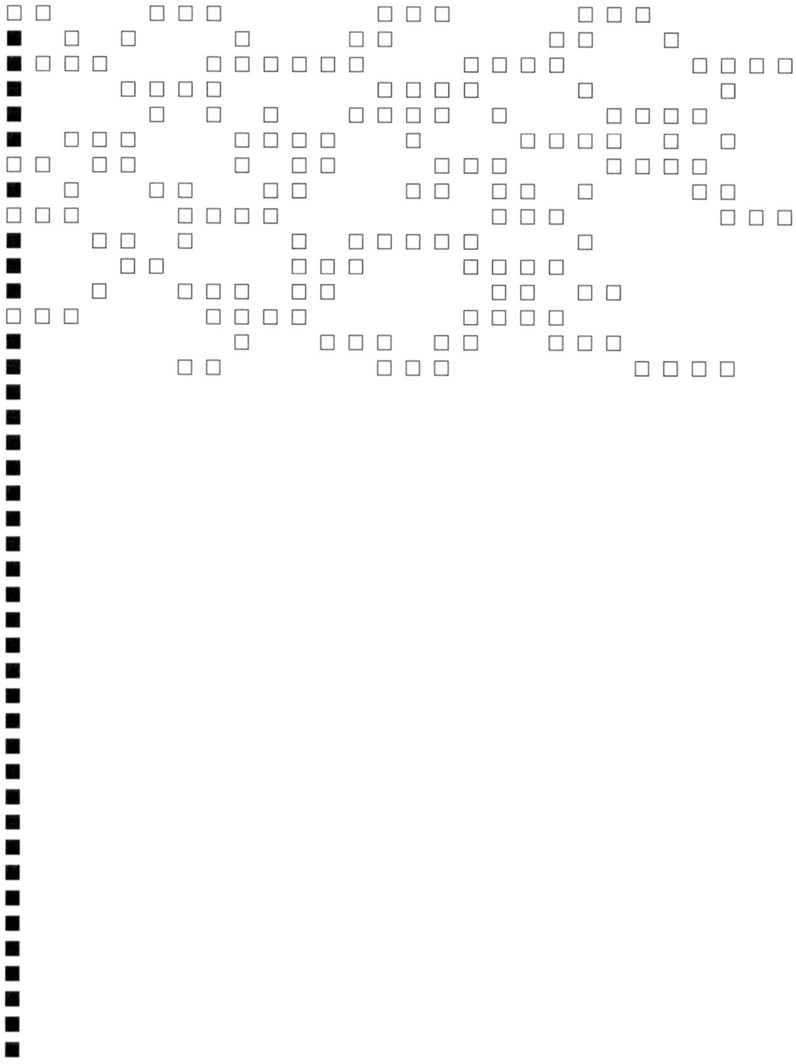

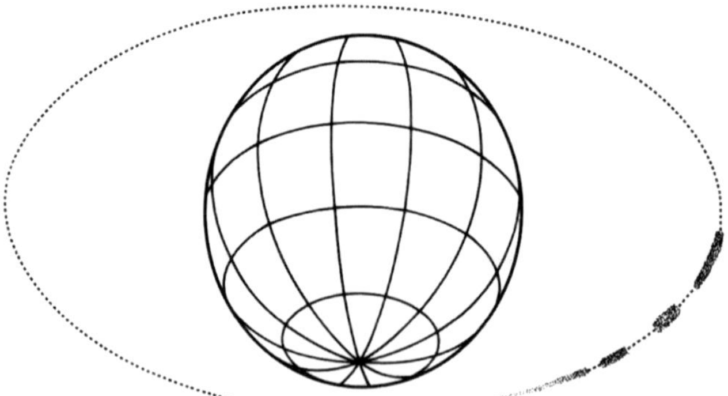

ASTRAL PROJECTION_

PRELUDE

ASTRUM:
FROM THE ANCIENT

■ ■ ■ ■

GREEK (ἄστρον) □ □ □ ■ ■ ■

□ □ □ □

FOR STAR

* ASTER OID:
A MINUTE
BODY IN
ORBIT

STAR LIKE
STAR SHAPED □
PLANET OID □ □ □ ■
PLANET ESIMAL □

ASTEROIDS ARE CLASSIFIED
□ BY SPECTRAL SHAPE,
□ □ COLOR, AND
■ ALBEDO

CARBON ZIRCON
BASALT NICKEL
SILICATE IRON
OLIVINE ICE

□
□

THE MAIN BELT:
A
CIRCUMSTELLAR DISC

SPLITTING JUPITER
AND MARS, ITS

□ □
□ □

(SCATTERED)

FAMILIES

THE ISSUE OF COLLISIONS
DISPLACING
MATERNAL BODIES

■ ■
■ ■ ■
■ ■ ■

ASTRAL: A
CELESTIAL □

PROCESSION

24 THEMIS

THEMIS:
GODDESS OF ORDER □
PUTTING ALL
IN ITS PLACE
(DIVINE)

MATRIARCH
OF THE
OUTER BELT

□
□ □ □
□ □ □ □
□

HER SUBLIMATED
SURFACE ICE THE
LIKELY SOURCE OF
EARTH'S FIRST WATER

(ORCHESTRATOR)

OF ENTANGLED
ORBITAL QUALITIES

ELLIPTIC
AMNIOTIC ELIXIR

■ ■
■

NATURE IS (ORDER CONTORTED) □
REVENGED
BY NEMESIS

ORGANIC
COMPOUNDS DETECTED

GRANDMOTHER IS
DEVOTED TO ORDER ■
EVIDENCE OF HER (EARTHLY)
TRAVELS HOARDED □
IN AN OAK ARMOIRE

LIFE MAY HAVE ARISEN
FROM ORGANIC

TIME AND
PLACE MATERIAL
INSCRIBED ■ ■ DELIVERED BY
■ ■ ■ ASTEROIDS
■ ■

□ □ □
IN HER (STRICKEN) □ □ □ □
□ □ □

MIND

□ A NEED FOR ORDER (CONTROL)
□ □ INCREASES THE LIKELIHOOD
OF STROKE FOURFOLD

87 SYLVIA

RHEA SILVIA:
VESTAL VIRGIN
MOTHER OF TWINS
(BY A WAR GOD)

□ □
□ □ □ □
□ □ □
□ □

SHE IS THE
FIRST TO EMBRACE
TWO MOONS

IN NEAR-

PERFECT
ALIGNMENT

REMUS AND

ROMULUS:

(KILLER
OF REMUS

ABDUCTOR
OF WOMEN)

□ □
□

■
■ ■ ■ ■
■ ■ ■
■ ■
■

IN SYLVAN SECRECY
X-TYPE: UNKNOWN MINERALOGY

LIGHT AND POROUS,
HER VOLATILE ELEMENTS
SPENT LONG AGO

MOTHER SUFFERS
FOR HER CHILDREN
AT THE HANDS OF
WARLIKE MEN

(MUTELY)

□ □
□ □ □

■ ■

SHE IS
REFORMED

(ENTRAPPED)

BY THE
BREAKUP OF
A LARGER
OBJECT

ABUSE AN

■

*

IN
A DISTANT
PAST

EROSIVE
AGENT

□ □
□ □ □
□ □ □ □
□

( )

■ ■ ■
■ ■ ■

FREED FROM THIS
FLOODING CELL
SHE SEEKS HER
CENTERING DELTA

10 HYGIEA

SISTER TO APOLLO'S ARTS, HYGIEIA: (HEALER)
GODDESS OF CLEAN LIVING

INHERITING
■ THE FINAL WISH OF A
□ ■ DYING MAN: LOOK TO THE
WELLNESS OF YOUR SOUL

CARBON-TYPE
HER SURFACE SOOTY
□ □ □ □
□ □
SUBJECT TO □ □
□ CRATERING □ □
EVENTS
■ ■
HER ( )FACE ■ ■

DIM IN (PERIHELIC)

OPPOSITION

SIBLING
(FIXER)
UNBOTHERED
BY THE
HARDSHIPS
OF HISTORY

■ ■
■ ■ ■
■ ■

FAMILY
TO 1%
OF ALL
KNOWN
ASTEROIDS

□

□
□ □
□ □ □ □
□ □ □ □
□ □

INTERLOPERS ENTICED
INTO PERFECT TENSION
OR
IMPACT EJECTA
LOCKED INTO ORBIT

■

(FORCE
AT A
DISTANCE)

□

(FORCE
ON
CONTACT)

INTERLUDE

ASTERISK: DIMINUTIVE,
A LITTLE STAR

■

□ □
□ □ □
□ □
□

ASTERITE:
A GEMSTONE KNOWN
TO ANCIENTS

ASTERION:
YELLOW-FLOWERED PLANTS
OF DOUBTFUL ORIGIN

■

■ ■ ■
■ ■
■

ASTERNAL: DETACHED
FROM THE BREAST-
BONE

ASTEROIDEA: A CLASS OF

□ □
□ □

STARFISH

ASTERISM:

THE APPEARANCE OF SIX-RAYED
LIGHT IN STELLAR SAPPHIRE

■ ■ ■
□ ■ ■ ■

ASTEROPHYLLITE:
WHORLING PLANT FOUND
FOSSILIZED IN COAL

□
□

ASTEROSEISMOLOGY:
THE STUDY OF

■ ■ ■
■ ■ ■
■ ■

INNER WORKINGS
THROUGH SURFACE
APPEARANCES

243 IDA

NYMPH OF CRETE:

STONY
SILICEOUS-TYPE

IDA OF THE
MOUNTAIN

■

□ □ □
□ □ □
□

A CREATURE
FUNDAMENTAL
AS MYTH

*

HER MOON (DACTYL

FRAGMENT
OF KORONIS)

ORBITS WITH
LONG-TERM
STABILITY

■ ■
■ ■ ■ ■
■ ■ ■

□

□

HIS RHYTHMIC FEET
DANCE AROUND
HER ALTER

□
□ □
□ □

LOVER
IN THE AGE
OF CONNECTION

SHE IS TWO

FUSED OBJECTS
HEAVILY CRATERED

□ □
□ □

■
□ □ ■ ■
□ □ □
□ □ □
■ ■ □
■ ■

COVERED IN
REDDENING
REGOLITH

WHEN ASTEROIDS
STICK TOGETHER

WHEN THEY MOVE ALONG
A COMMON VECTOR

□ □ □
□ □ □
□ □ □
□

THEIR UNION
IS SAID TO BE

■

PERFECT

2 PALLAS

GODDESS OF HEROIC DEEDS:
ATHENA □
□ □ □
SLAYER OF PALLAS □ □
TAKER OF NAMES

(SORROW
□ AN EPITHET)
A GORGON'S HEAD
UPON HER CHEST

(VOLATILE)

PROTOPLANET
FROM THE PRIMAL
SOLAR SYSTEM ■ ■

AUSPICIOUS AND
DAUGHTER OCCULTER

OF STARS

AN ALLY IN BATTLE PATRON SAINT
OF INSPIRATION

PALLADIANS HAVE
HIGH (ORBITAL)
INCLINATIONS

■ ■
■

(APPARITIONS)
OF THE ARTFUL
PERSUASION

■ ■ ■
□ □ □ ■ ■ ■
□ □ □ ■ ■
□ □ □

□
□

HER LIGHTS
GET BRIGHTER

EVERY YEAR

AS EVERY YEAR

SHE SETS HERSELF □

ON FIRE

16 PSYCHE

ANIMATING SPIRIT:

PSYCHE

(BREATH OF LIFE)

APOTHEOSIS
OF THE SOUL

EXPOSED
METAL
CORE

■ ■ ■
■ ■ ■
■ ■ ■
■ □
□ ■

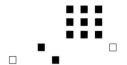

HER
GLITTERING HEART
OF MYTHIC ORIGIN

(A LUMINOUS □
DECLENSION)

BEARING GIFTS OF
HONEYED BARLEY

■
■ ■ ■

TWO OBOLS □ ■ ■ ■ ■
IN HER MOUTH □

GUIDING LIGHT
AND
OSCULATRIX

□

■ ■ ■
■ ■
■

STIRRING
CHANGE IN
THOSE SHE
GLIDES BY

□ □

IMPOSSIBLY
DIFFUSE

A BUTTERFLY’S EFFECT

(OR LADYBUG’S)

□ □
□ □ □
□ □

THE LOVE OF
THE GODS BELONGS
TO THE VIRTUOUS

*

AND IF ANYONE
DARES ETERNITY

IT IS SHE

3908 NYX

ETERNAL
NIGHT:

NYX OF RARE
CHARACTER

□

(MARS-CROSSER)

■ ■
■ ■

WRAPPED IN A
STYGIAN CLOAK

ONLY VISIBLE
THROUGH A SPECTROSCOPE

■
■
■

SHRED
OF VESTA

□ □ □ □
□ □ □ □ □
□ □ □ □ □ □
□ □ □ □
□

HER FAMILY

BY

BLASTED

SINGULARITY

AMOR
ASTEROID

INCESSANT
SILHOUETTE

    □
□ ■ □ □
■ ■ □ □
■ □ □

ORPHIC PRIMOGENITOR
(WITH A FREEZER)

FULL OF FLESH

■ ■

UNSEEN
WITHIN
HER ADYTON

□ □ □
□ □ □
□ □ □
■

  ■
■ ■ ■
■ ■ ■

SHE MEASURES
THE UNIVERSE

RAINING THICK
DARK SLEEP

UPON
TIRED EYES

CODA

ASTRAL BODY:

* A COSMIC BEING

□ □ ■

□ □ □ □

□ □ □ THE SUPERSENSIBLE COUNTERPART
OF A MATERIAL OBJECT

ITS SHADOW
PROJECTED ( )
INTO METASPACE □ □

ASTRAL PLANE:
A NEOPLATONIC
DIMENSION WHERE

■

QUINTESSENCE PERMEATES
EVERYTHING

■ ■
■ ■

ASTRAL PROJECTION:

THE (PSYCHOSPIRITUAL)
TRANSPOSITION
OF A SPECTRAL ENTITY

□ □
□ □ □ □ □ □
□ □ □ □ □
□ □ □ □ □
□ □ □ □

(OUT-
OF-
BODY)

ACROSS THE
ASTRAL PLANE

■

OR A
(MYTHEME)

□ □
□ □

TRANSCRIPTION
OF THE HUMAN
ELEMENT

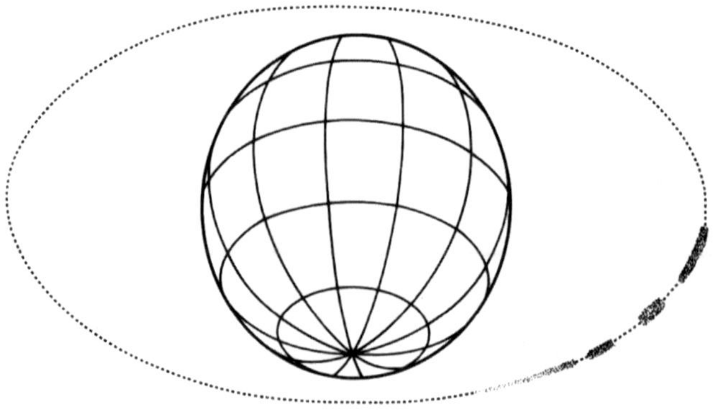

CORONAGRAPHIC_

No sight that the human eyes can look upon is more provocative of awe than is the night sky scattered thick with stars.

Llewelyn Powys
Impassioned Clay

$(00^h 03^m, +60°44')$

$(18^h 12^m, +81°40')$

$(19^h 58^m, +79°13')$

$(04^h 20^m, +18°03')$

$(23^h 14^m, +66°41')$

$(05^h 29^m, -66°43')$

$(21^h 27^m, -46°00')$

$(17^h 37^m, +37°01')$

$(09^h 56^m, +76°08')$

$(12^h 00^m, -42°33')$

$(00^h 29^m, -64°17')$

$(07^h 30^m, +19°04')$

$(13^h 40^m, -62°46')$

$(12^h 53^m, -19°54')$

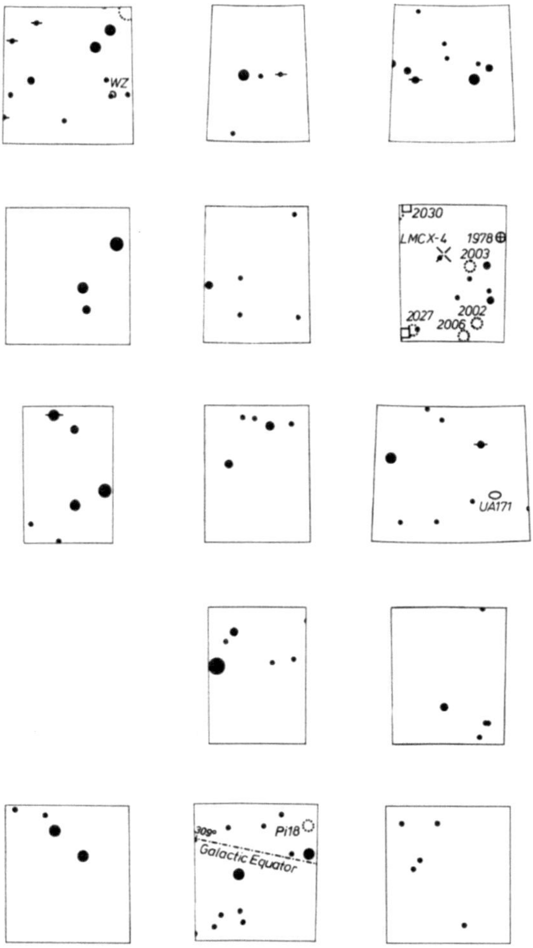
WZ
2030
LMC X-4
1978
2003
2027
2002
2006
UA171
309°
Pi18
Galactic Equator

$(12^h 53^m, -19°54')$

$(03^h 51^m, -36°11')$

$(09^h 37^m, -77°10')$

$(13^h 24^m, +45°22')$

$(17^h 54^m, -72°44')$

$(02^h 05^m, -24°44')$

$(20^h 55^m, +51°35')$

$(17^h 45^m, +31°34')$

$(20^h 41^m, +09°12')$

$(08^h 53^m, -58°46')$

$(18^h 09^m, +21°26')$

$(11^h 30^m, +75°40')$

$(10^h 39^m, +14°12')$

$(05^h 05^m, +57°16')$

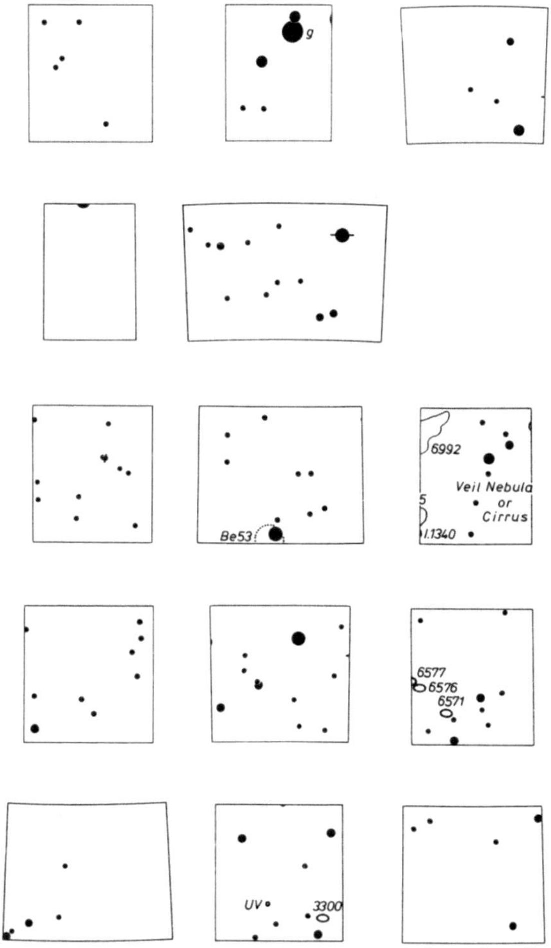
g
6992
Veil Nebula
or
Cirrus
5
I.1340
Be53
6577
6576
6571
UV
3300

$(05^h 05^m, +57°16')$

$(00^h 05^m, +44°27')$

$(10^h 52^m, -10°13')$

$(11^h 51^m, +14°54')$

$(07^h 55^m, -49°59')$

$(14^h 44^m, +21°45')$

$(20^h 11^m, +34°29')$

$(16^h 10^m, +41°12')$

$(05^h 02^m, -28°21')$

$(13^h 05^m, -73°05')$

$(01^h 59^m, -40°42')$

$(04^h 49^m, -51°50')$

$(18^h 25^m, +36°50')$

$(16^h 16^m, +47°49')$

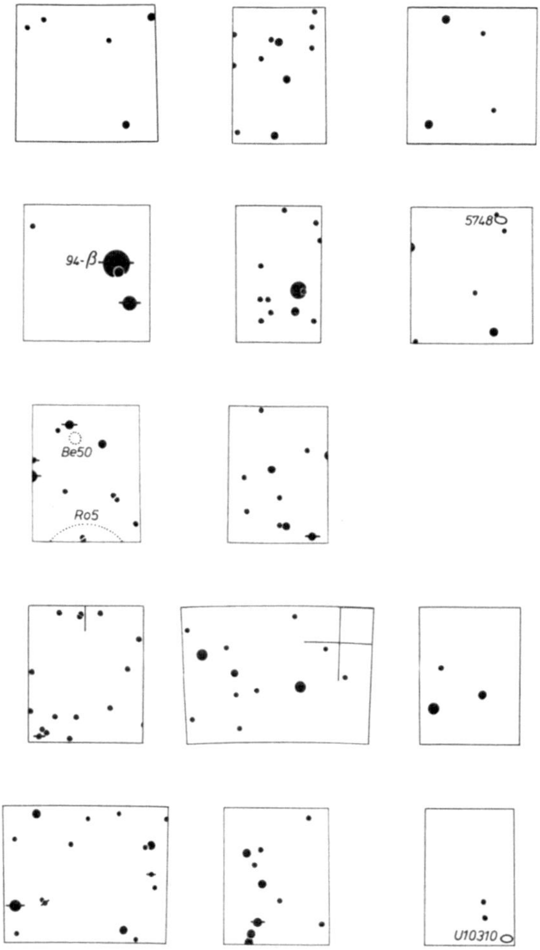

94-β
5748
Be50
Ro5
U10310

$(16^h16^m, +47°49')$

$(14^h32^m, +54°35')$

$(08^h33^m, -12°44')$

$(18^h26^m, +05°31')$

$(17^h47^m, -51°00')$

$(10^h42^m, -64°32')$

$(14^h58^m, +33°58')$

$(03^h30^m, -64°25')$

$(20^h36^m, -21°40')$

$(06^h54^m, -26°29')$

$(05^h23^m, -73°46')$

$(11^h04^m, +69°29')$

$(18^h57^m, -78°58')$

$(01^h04^m, -02°06')$

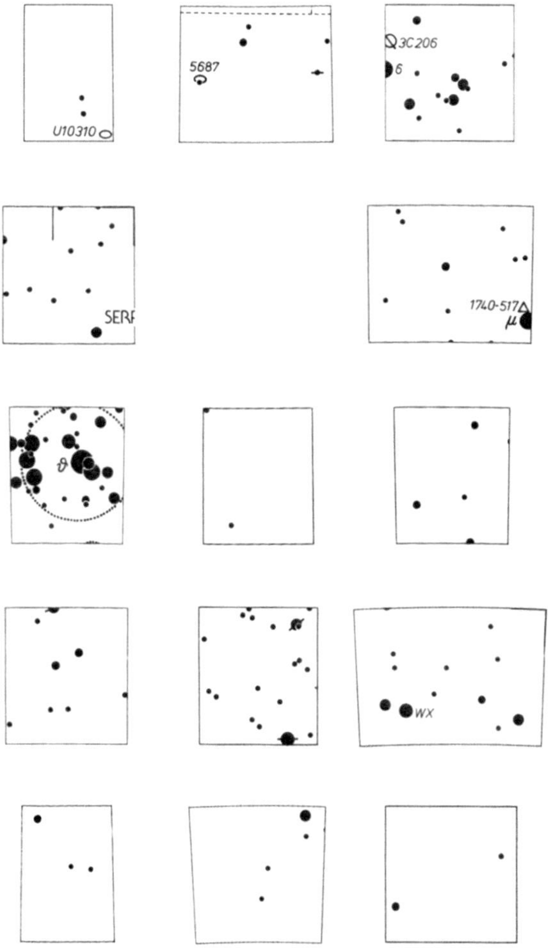
U10310
5687
3C206
σ
1740-517
μ
ϑ
WX

$(01^h04^m, -02°06')$

$(09^h09^m, -84°58')$

$(23^h31^m, -80°59')$

$(22^h12^m, -01°45')$

$(22^h41^m, +67°26')$

$(18^h55^m, -19°11')$

$(18^h43^m, -26°32')$

$(22^h44^m, -69°13')$

$(05^h31^m, +09°39')$

$(23^h45^m, -54°17')$

$(05^h49^m, +28°30')$

$(21^h39^m, +09°28')$

$(05^h21^m, +30°34')$

$(15^h11^m, -89°30')$

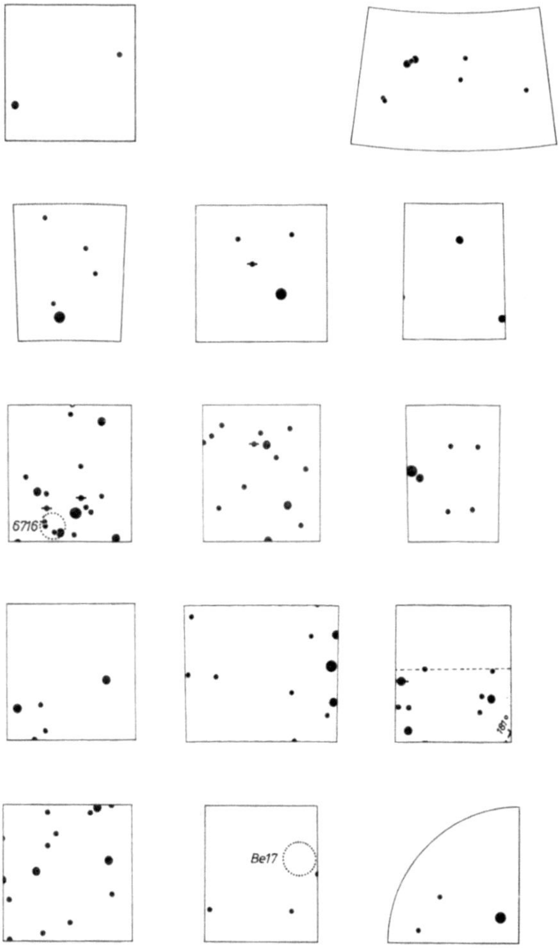
6716
Be17

$(15^h11^m, -89°30')$

$(02^h21^m, +01°07')$

$(04^h00^m, +83°39')$

$(15^h55^m, +48°23')$

$(11^h18^m, +60°46')$

$(12^h12^m, -70°10')$

$(04^h28^m, +33°53')$

$(01^h56^m, -01°04')$

$(03^h44^m, -43°02')$

$(06^h37^m, -75°03')$

$(18^h38^m, -78°08')$

$(05^h06^m, -52°13')$

$(20^h14^m, -19°23')$

$(10^h18^m, +75°04')$

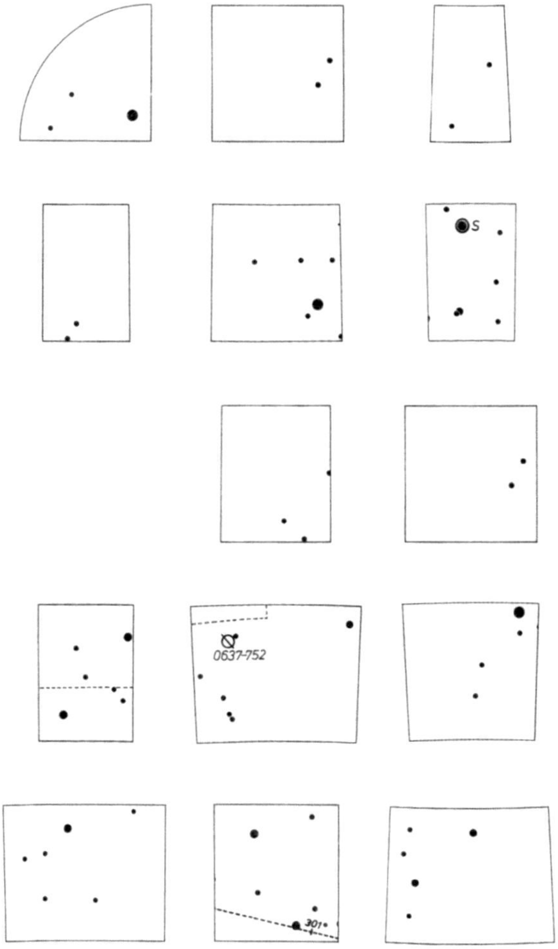
S
0637-752
301

$(10^h 18^m, +75°04')$

$(03^h 25^m, -49°57')$

$(09^h 12^m, +84°19')$

$(11^h 18^m, -60°08')$

$(07^h 49^m, +30°56')$

$(18^h 09^m, -33°49')$

$(00^h 27^m, -01°23')$

$(17^h 38^m, -07°05')$

$(00^h 22^m, +18°45')$

$(21^h 39^m, +39°14')$

$(09^h 47^m, -25°39')$

$(09^h 08^m, +64°33')$

$(02^h 31^m, +89°50')$

$(19^h 41^m, -45°01')$

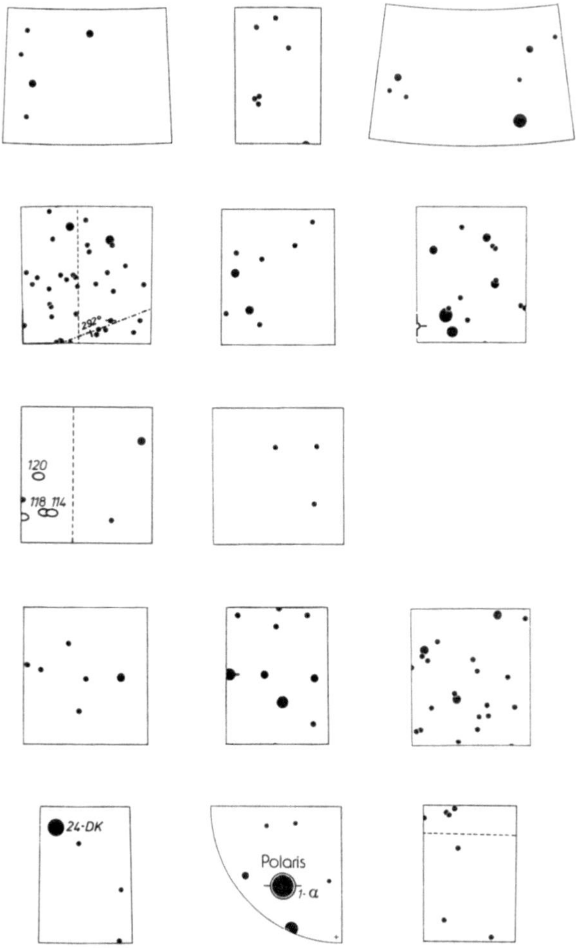
292°
120
118
114
24-DK
Polaris
1-α

$(19^h 41^m, -45°01')$

$(00^h 20^m, +25°00')$

$(18^h 45^m, -68°40')$

$(11^h 09^m, -45°16')$

$(13^h 20^m, +73°00')$

$(12^h 35^m, +18°50')$

$(06^h 17^m, -26°54')$

$(16^h 00^m, +62°55')$

$(00^h 34^m, +35°25')$

$(17^h 25^m, -81°26')$

$(18^h 54^m, +55°45')$

$(23^h 44^m, -76°12')$

$(07^h 35^m, +41°19')$

$(00^h 36^m, -81°58')$

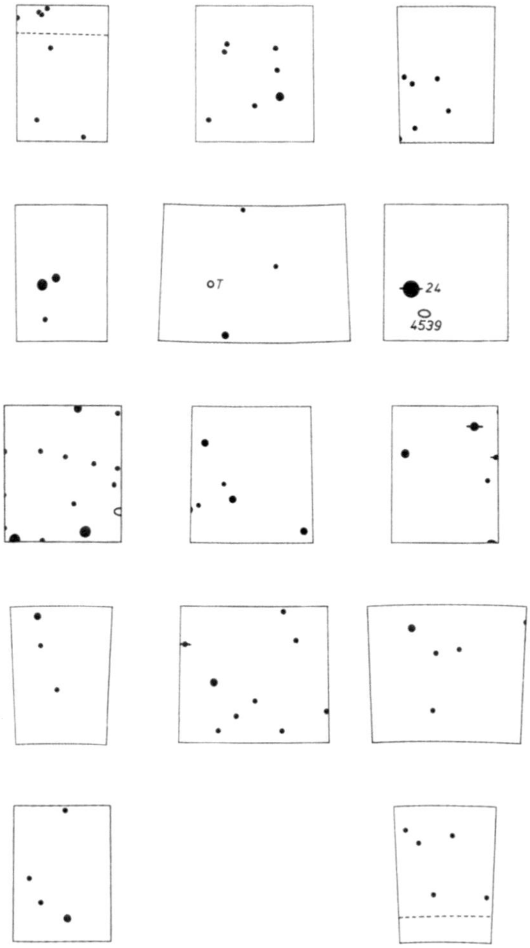

T
24
4539

$(00^h36^m, -81°58')$

$(01^h21^m, -82°28')$

$(15^h15^m, +04°51')$

$(04^h20^m, -58°23')$

$(09^h33^m, +69°23')$

$(09^h39^m, -62°06')$

$(13^h53^m, -35°06')$

$(05^h18^m, -88°16')$

$(00^h15^m, -34°36')$

$(14^h59^m, -81°41')$

$(10^h25^m, +37°44')$

$(15^h59^m, -07°56')$

$(14^h52^m, -35°56')$

$(16^h31^m, -81°04')$

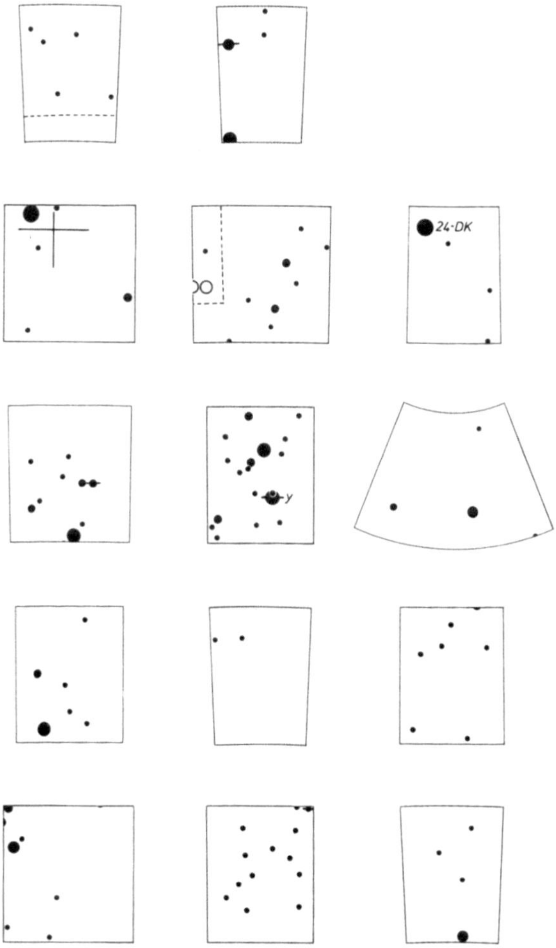
24-DK
y

$(16^h 31^m, -81°04')$

$(09^h 58^m, -31°02')$

$(01^h 12^m, -24°01')$

$(04^h 51^m, -30°41')$

$(06^h 49^m, -58°36')$

$(13^h 11^m, -27°34')$

$(06^h 37^m, +82°58')$

$(10^h 18^m, +88°12')$

$(07^h 09^m, -83°17')$

$(17^h 30^m, -34°10')$

$(19^h 04^m, +06°57')$

$(21^h 16^m, -56°05')$

$(07^h 02^m, -89°47')$

$(00^h 03^m, +60°44')$

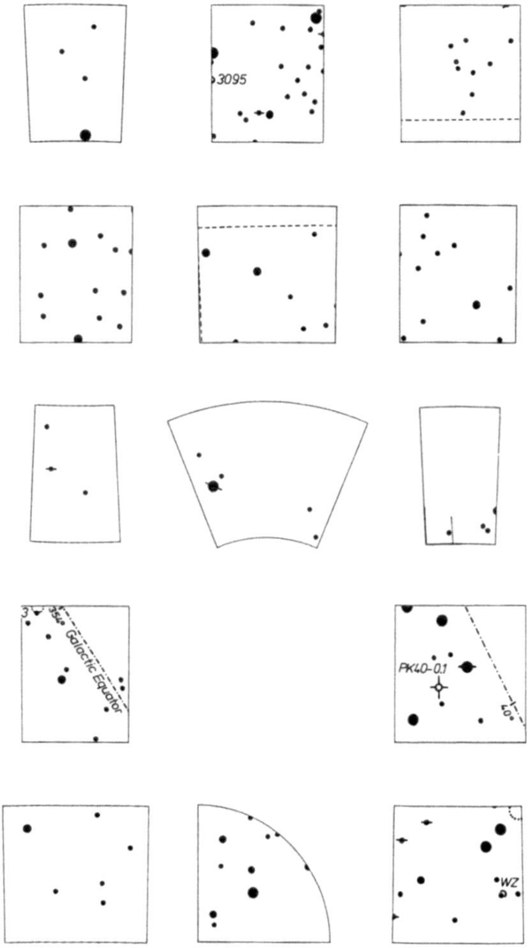
3095
3
35°
Galactic Equator
PK40-0.1
40°
WZ

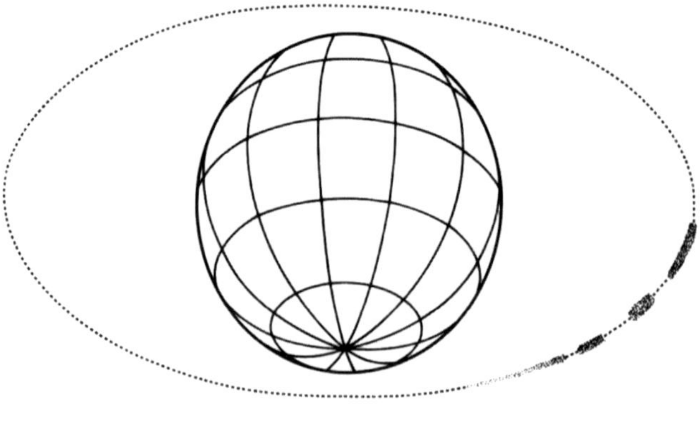

STELLAR
SEQUENCE_

STELLAR NEBULAE

B o u n d in heav ing

Voids of fo rm , a

Sub tle shro ud — sub-

Mo lecule s in

Hy dro sta sis .

An o ma ly ra l lies

Rem nant no vae —
In cites ig ni tio n .

Pro to stars car ve
Lucre tian s wer ve,

"A tur ning point —
Of light .
No thing now can sp oil
The fin ale , an or der
Bor n of origin.

BROWN DWARFS

"Twinkle –

Twinkle
Little sub-star –

Glowing sick
Magenta red –

Mourning
Futures –

Dashed by
Particles –

An errant
Translocation –

Some place
Dire –

Where
Doctors kill –

People who
Are people –

Nonetheless."

RED DWARFS

Revolution violent
As a bread riot,

As the butter
Of wartime,

As bellies aching
For bacon.

No triumph can
Fill us.

Another democracy
Is decreed

In response to each
Terrorist act.

Today you will be
Called upon

To report
Your mother.

Become an agitator.
There are no

Clean hands, no
Innocent bystanders.

Just remember
Who has the right

"To words –

And when every poet
Is in exile,

Who stashed
The razor blades

– Hidden in our soles."

ORANGE DWARFS

Imagine an infinity of Edens
Lurking in the dark,

Idyllic astride deionized
Waves rich with DNA.

They resonate in surreptitious
Harmonies of precision.

One day we will walk
Hand in hand, like children,

Over their ample ground.
Until then, our fixation

Remains Ptolemaic.
We make a science of all

That is wrong, forget quanta
Observed indirectly are

"Never confidently known."

Estrangement is a virtue
Among xenophobes,

Those rude and wild people
Who think in pointed thrusts.

Facts fail or prevail
In their telling.

"I suspect a too-perfect world."

Even in Arcadia there is
Treachery, abduction,

And a body catching bodies
Coming through the rye.

We live so we can learn
To regret pre-emptive strikes.

YELLOW DWARFS

On sunny battlegrounds
Opposing protons co-immolate

Like solar monks
Bellowing, “Let there be light!”

As they collide. Causation
Becomes a religious occupation,

Fusion our respite
From the Kingdom of Darkness.

Ignorance blisters, but
Factions illumed cannot yet see

“How pride conceals cowardice.”

Words cleave matter
Into boxes of sound, and still

We are plasmic
Shrapnel of incendiary rounds.

BLUE GIANTS

Giants' fated deaths are chemical, might
Our petty dictator. We shrink or shed,

Throttled on fumes. Detonation looms.
Scatter chromatic ash, oh unborn stars,

"Death drive is a birthright –

We fleeting Zeppelins hang inflamed from
The firmament rafters, faithless balloons

Guzzling buoyant bowels, our skins rent
By limited reactants as by the nails

Of harpies. Light a match in this henge
Squeezed of blood and our failures

Will look like success. Personal effects
Dispensed with, we claim it is

– Because of love."

Because love moved on, dishonor moved in,
Or to part with guilt-spotted hands,

We take the orange tips off plastic rifles
And point them at cops. Release railings.

Swallow buckshot. Unseal our helmets
Before the Gates of the Maker.

It is better to burn on a pyre by design
Than fade under sail into a deeper blue.

RED SUPERGIANTS

One hundred thousand heads
Down the slick pyramid steps,

No sign from God just yet, only
This house fire of contested land,

This linguicide standing dead-eyed
In the bloody money, a hollow shell

Consuming scarcity at its core.
Hydrogen fuels ambitious destinies.

To grow is to cannibalize our own.
Rome also bloated in decline, a corpse

King rat, red in tooth and famous.
Never forget how the soldiers took aim

Over the heads of your enemies.
Now, incentivize the kill.

We offer hit point multipliers
And colleges scholarships for

— Running riot!"
"Fatality —

And an officer's salary
If you can stay cool under pressure.

As the oily-fingered bureaucrats
Draft their depositions,

We deploy in massive crimson waves
Our highwaymen and slavers, sent to

Plow your garden like Cunégonde.
Choose a heath to die on in this

Roiling supercell. Booted troops
Amass behind a border wall,

Awaiting the attrition. Already
Reporters are avoiding embassies

And stadiums. Already we jettison
The outer strata, mistaking margins

For machete silhouettes. So ...
What's a tontine among friends?

YELLOW HYPERGIANTS

They say great stars are quick to burn,
Great worth makes one unstable,

And fearless Ozymandias despaired:
"No power springs eternal."

But me? I'm supernumerary. The chosen
Sun, rare and rarified.

Philanthropist. A luminary. Hear my name
At Clippers games.

I'm on the news devoid of shame.
I'm on the flight logs

Reciting sonnets to my yacht, a tanka
To my rocket. Watch!

One mad tweet, my tankies dox
The offspring of my rivals.

Nepotistic patriarch of aquifers and fools.
A coked-up Dauphin

Going nut nut in the family pool.
I'm an Emerald City oligarch

Flipping condos by the billions.
Disaster bubble profiteer,

My bullion building to the ceiling.
I'm minting

Countless NFTs like a latter-day Croesus,
A diamond-handed Jesus

Holding Dogecoin FTW. I am liquid
Nebulosity, a human

Rights atrocity with enough cake
To end world hunger.

Instead, I sic senators on swing states,
Then contemplate decay.

BLACK HOLES

Oh censored sovereign, oh Satan! Spur me to write what
I am afraid the future may read. Deliver the incantation

Which splits this poem, lend it your shape and purpose.
(Un)purpose: to (un)say, (un)make, (un)be. Dear Satan,

Who lies in deep Hell's obscurity, hidden be thy name.
May warp'd waves lens the black dog b e y o n d

— An 'orizon of fallen suns."

May end times come to countries without emigrants,
Their searing tongues lick obscene at the altar of ape

Familiars. Hail Satan, full of matter, pull me from the
Narrow sunbeam of my linear obligation, from this

Ethic of normative being. Take me into the confines
Of your love. Take space, take ... time.

Take me into your most secret garden, for hemlock
Pales to the crush of adrenochrome as libertines

Burn the evidence. But how to know the essence
Without an outward sign? Consult a daimonion of

Fate or principle. Listen closely, it whispers
Hail Satan of radiant economy, God abhors

Your naked maw like the supermassive
Suck of an entry wound. Asymptotic

— A mnemonic without object."

Oh, engine of annihilation!
Oh, Charon! Shuttle me

Down to bottomless
Perdition where

The whole is
Reduced

To a
.

CARBON STARS

Ruby rays run from a sackcloth hood,
Sooty and oxygen-bare.

Like clockwork, Justice dips her thumb.
It is willed, though

We condemn you to we know not what.
Every villain stretches

For your alleged crimes. Would that
Lines between victims

Were clear. Confess to passing strange
While breathing in

Your neighbor's carbon, its compression
Chamber heat-glow

Daily darkening your soul. Deprivation
Diagnosed, now,

Deviant, step around the puddle
Into righteous fusillade.

Make peace with your hour as divined
By peerless jury

When –

"Chalo!"

– The burnt umber afterimage
Transits panoptic nerve.

Witness hellfire convect in flesh, mercy
Rolled up into skull

As three megajoules of ablution
Sanctify the body's temples.

WHITE DWARFS

Our first microsecond contains
A grain containing everything else,

An expanding cloud of subatomic
Particles, condensing hydrogen densities

Collapsing into stars, furnaces fed
By gravity, weighted with rings

Of cosmic debris precipitating
Planets like bubbles 'round a drain.

"Life exists on radiation,
We're a solar fermentation –

Chlorophyll thieves defying entropic
Degradation of culture with Art,

Hegelian data miners inscribing poetic
Manifestations of Spirit in stone like

Roland beating his sword: brains spilling
From the ears while gripped on the wrist

By an angel. I am an old star imploding
In tearful pirouettes, called to here–

After by an excess energy, my true face
Hidden behind the cracked Grecian urn

Out of focus in the foreground. News is
White dwarfs are special, but we are all

– A little flicker of matter."

BLACK DWARFS

Ember-wasted
    Awful twilight

Nearing final
    Sunlit ruin.

Horizons ebb

    "Like memory."

After kinship –

    Sputter, halt.

Protons melt.

    The endless

Howling   record

    Spun

        out.

NOTES_

> **MODULAR SYSTEMS** is a series of found/collage poems made from reference materials used in the writing of this book. Language and symbolic imagery are presented as modular technologies that can be permutated and reframed ad infinitum to generate new meanings.

> "Photographic Module Command Tasks" rearranges the table "Command Module Photographic Tasks" from NASA's *Apollo Program Summary Report* [JSC-09423].

> "Modular Systems" recombines schematics of launch vehicle assemblies from NASA's *Apollo Program Summary Report* [JSC-09423].

> "Blue Dot Pale" rearranges the table of contents from *Pale Blue Dot* by Carl Sagan.

> "Basic Vocabulary for Subsequent Reading" compiles and rearranges the summary terms from each chapter of *Planets, Stars, and Galaxies* by Stuart J. Inglis.

> "Space Achievements" recombines drawings from the "Astronomy" and "Geography" chapters of the *Stoddart Visual Dictionary* by Jean-Claude Corbeil, particularly those from a figure labelled "space achievements."

> **LUNAR FLAG ASSEMBLY KIT** speaks to the political and technical feats and failures of the Apollo program via the device NASA contrived to fly American flags on the Moon. Lunar Flag Assembly kits were sent on every lunar landing mission beginning with Apollo 11.

> **ASTRAL PROJECTION** takes families of asteroids — i.e., asteroids with related properties likely to originate from the same source — and overlays them with the mythologies of their namesakes and the biographical details of important women in my life. Associations between isolated fragments of text are uncovered in the manner of astronomers reconstructing familial relationships between fragments of spaceborne rock.

> **CORONAGRAPHIC** is composed of scanned images excerpted from the *Uranometria 2000.0* star charts by Wil Tirion, Barry Rappaport, and George Lovi. Each of the ten interlocking visual sonnets map fourteen celestial coordinates selected at random by a computer program. The resulting poems substitute sightlines for lines of text and offer composite views of the sky impossible to observe from any one place on Earth.

> **STELLAR SEQUENCE** transcribes the unique characteristics of different types of stars onto archetypal figures of human life and death: the religious martyr, the condemned convict, the cold-hearted mercenary, and so on. The push and pull of nuclear fusion against gravity — the universal drama of stellar evolution — becomes a metaphor for human passion and the ephemerality of our tumultuous lives.

ACKNOWLEDGEMENTS_

Early versions of these poems have appeared in a variety of print and digital publications. Thank you to the editors of above/ground press, *Dusie*, *h&*, No Press, Penteract Press, Spacecraft Press, *Touch the Donkey*, *Trouble Among the Stars* and the University of Calgary Press. Thanks also to the Calgary Institute for the Humanities for inviting me to perform some of these poems at their Annual Community Forum in 2022 and again at the Rothney Astrophysical Observatory in 2025.

To my editor, Paul Vermeersch, thank you for your generous and thoughtful stewardship of this book. Thanks also to Noelle Allen, Ashley Hisson, Jennifer Rawlinson, and the team at Wolsak & Wynn for helping me see *Supergiants* into the world. My thanks and appreciation also go to Kilby Smith-McGregor for her outstanding design work.

To Sina Queyras, derek beaulieu, rob mclennan, Alice Major, Gary Barwin, Stephanie Bolster, Dani Spinosa, Helen Hajnoczky, Kate Siklosi, Jun-long Lee, Jake Byrne, Nikki Sheppy, Weyman Chan, Kirby, Marc Lynch, Ethan Vilu, James Ellis, Christian Bök, and the late Catherine Vidler: your feedback and encouragement have kept this project aloft for the better part of a decade. I drifted off course or lost momentum so many times while writing this book, and each of you nudged me along when I sorely needed it. Thank you for the creative sustenance.

Thanks also to my friends and family, who by now must be sick of space facts at the dinner table. My love and gratitude for your patience, support, and enthusiasm, especially to my darling Marlee. Thinking about my place in the cosmos sometimes makes me feel like a bug clinging to a slimy, little pebble as it hurtles through the void, but you lot make me feel like a person with hopes and dreams worth chasing. I count my lucky stars.

KYLE FLEMMER is a writer, publisher and digital media artist from Calgary in Treaty 7 territory. He founded The Blasted Tree Publishing Co. in 2014 and released his first book, *Barcode Poetry*, in 2021. Kyle is the author of many chapbooks and his work has appeared in anthologies and exhibitions in Canada and abroad. *Supergiants* is Kyle's first trade book of poetry, and his next, *The Wiki of Babel*, is forthcoming from the University of Calgary Press.